W9-AYO-247

Recipes from Around the World

by Jules Bond

BARRON'S
Woodbury, New York • London • Toronto • Sydney

All inquiries should be addressed to:

Barron's Educational Series, Inc.
113 Crossways Park Drive
Woodbury, New York 11797

International Standard Book
No. 0-8120-5604-3
Library of Congress Catalog Card
No. 84-6344

**Library of Congress Cataloging in Publication
Data**
Bond, Jules Jerome.
    Recipes from around the world.

    Includes index.
    1. Cookery. I. Title.
TX725.A1B674   1984   641.59   84-6344
ISBN 0-8120-5604-3

PRINTED IN HONG KONG
4 5 6 7   490   9 8 7 6 5 4 3 2 1

Credits

Photography
Color photographs: Karen Leeds
Food styling: Yoshiko Loomis
Photo stylist: Linda Peacock

Author Jules Bond is the author of over 20
cookbooks.

Cover and book design Milton Glaser, Inc.

Series editor Carole Berglie

INTRODUCTION

In the past two decades Americans have discovered a new world—the world of the great cuisines of other countries, of other continents. In this new book we offer you a sampling of these cuisines, to enable you to travel gastronomically around the globe.

Some cuisines have been known here for a long time. Early settlers were from England, thus the fundamental basis for our food is solid English cooking. But soon after the English came the French, the Spanish, and, through the decades, succeeding waves of other immigrants. These immigrants brought from their homelands the foods and flavors of their past, and these tastes gradually became part of what we today call the mixed bag of "American food." Thus, the dishes that characterize British, French, Spanish, German, and Scandinavian foods are not completely new to us. German and Scandinavian cuisine became known in many parts of America, particularly the Midwest. Spanish or Mexican cooking strongly influenced the taste of the Southwest and southern California. In the last century, Chinese laborers brought many Cantonese dishes with them. And, of course, the country's big cities have always had a smattering of foreign restaurants, from the more expected French and Italian to those representing the lesser-known Third-World countries.

There's a new, all-consuming interest, however, in the many varied regional dishes from other countries. We now seek out the specialties of the French provinces, the contrasting flavors of northern Italy, and the foods of Sichuan and other Chinese provinces. Japanese food has also become popular in America, as have the cuisines of Thailand, Indonesia, India, Pakistan, and many other countries. This book takes you on a gastronomic tour through many lesser-known parts of the world, from Scandinavia to Portugal and Spain, from France across Europe to the Middle East and India, from Indonesia to Japan, China and Korea, from the Caribbean to Chile.

Some years ago it was difficult, if not impossible, to find many of the ingredients for even the simplest "foreign food," especially outside of metropolitan areas. Now supermarkets across the nation carry extensive stocks of Hispanic, Chinese, Japanese, and other oriental foods on their shelves. You should have little problem locating the ingredients used in this collection of recipes; they are slightly different—offering you a taste of the unusual—while utilizing readily available ingredients.

All countries have their preferences, not only for certain seasonings, but also very often for the way to cook and present them. We find that the farther north one travels, the more substantial the dishes—rich and heavy soups, stews, and roasts. The fats used in cooking are often lard and other animal fats. Butter and cream are lavishly used in the cuisine of northern France, while sour cream is important in Central Europe.

In areas farther south, there is always less emphasis on meat. Since butter is perishable and its production depends on cattle herds, oil is the favorite cooking medium, especially olive oil. Vegetables and salads of many kinds are important in the daily menu. More spices, herbs, and condiments are used in cooking. And garlic is a favorite ingredient in most countries with warm or tropical climates.

It seems the hotter the climate, the hotter the food. Central and South Americans thrive on a seemingly endless variety of hot peppers. Southern India and countries of Southeast Asia serve many "incendiary" dishes; so do some of China's provinces. For those who would like to put out the conflagration started by some fiery curries, here is a tip from India, where a bowl of plain yogurt is often served with curries. After a few mouthfuls of curry, a spoonful of smooth yogurt is a most cooling and pleasant intermezzo.

The type of food preferred and most often served in many countries is dictated not only by climate, but frequently by the location of the country. Japan, for example, is surrounded by water and short of arable land, thus the Japanese emphasize the consumption of seafood. Fish and shellfish are the sources of some of their best dishes, including broiled seafood as well as raw, sparkling fresh fish, delicately sliced and artistically presented as sashimi and sushi.

Portugal is another country where seafood is a most important item on the daily menu. Portugal is a fairly thin strip of land with many miles of Atlantic seacoast, and its foods are some of the best fish dishes of Europe.

Methods of cooking and preparation are strongly influenced by the geographical location of a country. In cold climates one finds many dishes that require long simmering on the stove, a stove that in many houses is the prime source of heat. In tropical climates the time expended in cooking is usually quite short. Countries where fuel is scarce, in many regions of China for instance, highly fuel-efficient methods of cooking have been developed; the wok permits quick cooking, for example. Grilling food over charcoal can often be traced to the nomadic influence of the past—such as in many of the great broiled dishes of the Middle East and North Africa.

No special equipment or utensils are necessary for these recipes. For cooking some oriental dishes, a wok may be helpful—millions of Americans own them these days—but a good skillet can be used instead. A few saucepans, a skillet, tight-fitting covers, some good sharp knives, a strainer, and a wooden spoon or two are all that is needed to prepare the dishes in this book. I find chopsticks among the most useful stirrers in a kitchen.

Staples used in these recipes are found in every average kitchen. Oil—corn or peanut oil and a bottle of good olive oil—should be in everybody's pantry. There should also be a good vinegar: white wine vinegar and oriental rice vinegar are the ones I prefer, especially rice vinegar for very delicate dishes.

Herbs and spices are mostly the standard ones on everybody's spice shelf. There are, however, many sins committed in the storage of herbs and spices. They should be stored in a cool, dark place in tightly closed containers. The often-used "convenient" place for herbs and spices, right over the stove, is certain to destroy their flavors in a matter of weeks. Red spices, especially good Hungarian paprika, should always be kept in the refrigerator to preserve flavor and color for many months. Herbs should be replaced every few months to have a fragrant, fresh-tasting supply on hand. Fresh gingerroot is now available in most markets; powdered ginger is not an adequate substitute. The soy sauce mentioned in these pages is the Japanese variety—Kikkoman brand is preferred.

Many of the dishes in this book can be started or prepared in advance. One of the best time-saving tricks of the trade—French chefs call it "mise en place," or, assembly of all ingredients—is to have everything ready, cleaned and assembled in the needed quantities, as well as the utensils you need before you start to cook. Most of the recipes take very little time and effort to prepare. None of them is difficult for anyone who cooks, even only occasionally.

Cooking times indicated are, of course, approximate. The actual time will vary somewhat, depending on the quality and amount of food being prepared. The time needed for preparation is also approximate, depending on the cook, who may have more or less experience in handling foods.

UNDERSTANDING THE RECIPE ANALYSES

For each recipe in this book, you'll note that we have provided data on the quantities of protein, fat, sodium, carbohydrates, and potassium, as well as the number of calories (kcal) per serving. If you are on a low-calorie diet or are watching your intake of sodium, for example, these figures should help you gauge your eating habits and help you balance your meals. Bear in mind, however, that the calculations are fundamentally estimates, and are to be followed only in a very general way. The actual quantity of fat, for example, that may be contained in a given portion will vary with the quality of meat you buy or with how much care you take in skimming off cooking fat. The analyses are based on the number of portions given as the yield for the recipe, but if the yield reads, "4 to 6 servings," we indicate which number of servings (4, for example) was used to come up with the final amounts.

YIELD

4 servings

Per serving

calories 404, protein 50 g,
fat 18 g, sodium 565 mg,
carbohydrates 6 g,
potassium 689 mg

TIME

15 minutes preparation
5 minutes cooking

INGREDIENTS

2 dozen jumbo shrimp
3 tablespoons olive oil
2 tablespoons butter
1 large clove garlic, crushed
2 anchovy fillets, mashed
1 tablespoon tomato paste
1 teaspoon lemon juice
1/3 cup dry white wine
1 tablespoon minced fresh parsley
Salt and pepper to taste

Shell ① and devein shrimp ②. In a skillet, heat oil and butter. Sauté shrimp over moderately high heat for about 2 to 3 minutes, until they turn pink. Turn them once during cooking. Do not overcook. Remove shrimp from skillet and keep warm.

Add all other ingredients to skillet. Blend well and cook over high heat while stirring ③ for about 2 minutes, until sauce is smooth and reduced by about half. Place shrimp on a serving dish, spoon sauce over, and serve.

YIELD

4 to 6 servings

Per serving (4)
calories 794, protein 63 g,
fat 48 g, sodium 399 mg,
carbohydrates 25 g,
potassium 711 mg

TIME

20 minutes preparation
1½ hours cooking

INGREDIENTS

1 roasting chicken, about 4 pounds
1 tablespoon lemon juice
Salt and pepper to taste
2 tablespoons butter
1 small onion, minced
1 small clove garlic, minced
1½ cups cooked white rice
2 tablespoons chopped fresh parsley
2 tablespoons currants
¼ cup pine nuts (pignoli)

⅓ cup chopped walnuts
1 egg, lightly beaten
1 tablespoon tomato paste
¼ cup chicken broth, canned or fresh
1 tablespoon olive oil

Rinse chicken, inside and out, with cold water ①. Pat dry. Sprinkle inside with lemon juice and salt and pepper. Chop the raw liver. Preheat oven to 350 degrees.

In a skillet, heat butter and sauté the chopped chicken liver with the onion and garlic until light golden, about 2 minutes. Remove from heat and blend with all other ingredients except olive oil. Stuff chicken with the mixture ②, close the opening, and truss ③.

Rub chicken with olive oil, place in a roasting pan, and add about ⅓ cup water to the pan. Place in hot oven and roast for about 1½ hours, until tender and nicely browned. Baste with pan juices during cooking and add more water if needed. Allow to rest a few minutes before carving.

YIELD

4 servings

Per serving
calories 499, protein 39 g,
fat 29 g, sodium 457 mg,
carbohydrates 22 g,
potassium 964 mg

TIME

20 minutes preparation
1 hour, 30 minutes
  cooking

INGREDIENTS

1½-pound piece brisket of beef
¼ cup all-purpose flour
2 tablespoons butter
1 cup beef broth, canned or fresh
1 large onion, coarsely chopped
3 carrots, pared and sliced
1 parsnip, pared and sliced
⅓ cup chopped fresh parsley
2 stalks celery (white part only), sliced

Salt and pepper
¾ cup sour cream
1 tablespoon chopped fresh dill leaves
  or 2 teaspoons dillweed

Cut meat into ¾-inch-thick slices ①, then dredge lightly with flour ②. In a saucepan, heat butter. Brown meat quickly on both sides, then add broth, cover and cook gently for 1 hour. Add vegetables, season with salt and pepper, and add a little more broth if too dry. Cover and simmer for another 30 minutes.

Correct seasoning and remove from heat. Stir in sour cream ③, sprinkle with dill, and serve.

YIELD

4 to 6 servings

Per serving (4)
calories 418, protein 39 g,
fat 23 g, sodium 275 mg,
carbohydrates 11 g,
potassium 630 mg

TIME

15 minutes preparation
1 hour resting
1 hour cooking

INGREDIENTS

1 pound lean ground lamb
3/4 pound lean ground beef
2 thick slices white bread, soaked in
   milk and squeezed dry
1/3 cup grated onion
2 cloves garlic, minced
1 egg, lightly beaten
1 1/2 teaspoons curry powder, or to
   taste
1 teaspoon caraway seeds

1 1/2 teaspoons lemon juice
2 tablespoons chopped fresh parsley
1 tablespoon dillweed
Salt and pepper to taste

4

Blend all ingredients. Pack the mixture into a loaf pan ① and let stand for one hour before cooking.

Preheat the oven to 350 degrees.

Place the loaf pan in a larger pan ②, add water about 1 inch deep ③, and bake in hot oven for 1 hour. Let cooked loaf sit for 5 minutes before slicing.

5

YIELD

4 servings

Per serving
calories 484, protein 40 g,
fat 24 g, sodium 2991 mg,
carbohydrates 21 g
potassium 794 mg

TIME

15 minutes preparation
30 minutes cooking

INGREDIENTS

½ cup dry red wine
¼ cup port wine
3 tablespoons red currant jelly
1 teaspoon dry mustard
1 teaspoon lemon juice
2 teaspoons cornstarch
1 ham steak, about 2 pounds

In a small saucepan, blend all ingredients except ham, and cook, stirring, over low heat until the sauce is clear and thickened ①.

Preheat oven to 325 degrees.

Place ham on a rack in a baking pan ②, then coat both sides with the sauce. Bake in hot oven for 30 minutes. Brush with sauce several times during cooking ③. When done, spoon remaining sauce over ham and serve.

YIELD

4 to 6 servings

Per serving (4)
calories 416, protein 40 g,
fat 17 g, sodium 270 mg,
carbohydrates 25 g,
potassium 1143 mg

TIME

30 minutes preparation
2 hours, 15 minutes
    cooking

INGREDIENTS

2½ pounds stewing lamb (breast or
    neck), with bones
3 lean, meaty beef shortribs
6 cups water, or 3 cups canned
    chicken broth mixed with 3 cups
    water
1 large onion, minced
2 large carrots, pared and grated
3 stalks celery, trimmed and diced
1 leek, trimmed, washed, and sliced
1 parsnip, pared and diced

¼ cup barley, rinsed and drained
1 small bay leaf
3 tablespoons chopped fresh parsley
½ teaspoon dried leaf thyme
Salt and pepper to taste

Rinse lamb and shortribs. Place meat in a kettle or saucepan, add water, cover, bring to a boil, and simmer for 1 hour. Add remaining ingredients, cover again, and simmer an additional hour.

Remove meat from kettle; let cool slightly. Take meat off the bones ①, shred or dice the meat ②, and return to kettle. Simmer broth for another 10 minutes. Skim fat off the surface ③ and serve.

7

YIELD

4 servings

Per serving
calories 416, protein 38 g,
fat 27 g, sodium 366 mg,
carbohydrates 4 g,
potassium 866 mg

TIME

15 minutes preparation
10 minutes cooking
8 hours chilling

INGREDIENTS

4 tablespoons butter
2 pounds fish fillets (flounder,
  snapper, or other firm white fish)
¼ cup olive oil
¼ cup tarragon vinegar
¼ cup orange juice
1 tablespoon lime juice
1 teaspoon grated orange rind
2 tablespoons minced scallions (white
  part only)

1 clove garlic, crushed
2 tablespoons chopped green bell
  pepper
1 tablespoon chopped canned
  pimiento
1 bay leaf
Salt and pepper to taste
Dash of Tabasco (optional)

Heat butter in a skillet, then brown the fish fillets quickly on both sides ①. Remove fish carefully to a serving dish ②. Combine all other ingredients. Pour mixture over the fish ③. Cover dish tightly with foil or plastic wrap, and chill for about 8 hours. Serve cold.

YIELD

4 servings

Per serving
calories 556, protein 40 g,
fat 42 g, sodium 279 mg,
carbohydrates 3 g,
potassium 389 mg

TIME

20 minutes preparation
4 hours marinating
1 hour cooking

INGREDIENTS

1 chicken, about 3 pounds, cut in
  serving pieces
4 tablespoons olive oil
2 tablespoons grated onion
1 large clove garlic, crushed
½ teaspoon dried leaf thyme
½ teaspoon dried marjoram
½ teaspoon ground coriander
Peel of 1 lemon, grated
Juice of 1 lemon

1 teaspoon paprika
Salt and pepper to taste
3 tablespoon butter
2 tablespoons minced fresh parsley

In a bowl, blend all ingredients except butter and parsley. Rub the mixture well into the chicken pieces ① and let marinate for 4 hours. Turn the pieces in the marinade a few times ②.

Preheat the oven to 350 degrees.

Butter a baking dish, place chicken in 1 layer in the dish, and dot with pats of butter ③. Bake in hot oven for about 1 hour or until chicken is tender. Baste a few times with remaining marinade. Sprinkle chicken with parsley when serving.

YIELD

4 servings

Per serving
calories 462, protein 20 g,
fat 40 g, sodium 849 mg,
carbohydrates 4 g,
potassium 455 mg

TIME

15 minutes preparation
20 minutes cooking

INGREDIENTS

1 pound sirloin or flank steak
2 tablespoons oil
1 medium onion, sliced paper thin
2 cloves garlic, minced
2 tablespoons shredded gingerroot
½ cup shredded celery (white part
    only)
½ cup beef broth, canned or fresh
2 tablespoons soy sauce
Black pepper to taste

Slice meat into julienne strips about 3 inches long ①. In a heavy skillet, heat oil and sauté onion until light golden ②. Add garlic, and sauté for another half minute. Add beef strips ③, stir well, then add remaining ingredients. Bring to a boil, then simmer for about 15 minutes until sauce has thickened and meat is cooked.

Serve with boiled white rice.

YIELD

4 servings

Per serving
calories 558, protein 38 g,
fat 38 g, sodium 505 mg,
carbohydrates 16 g,
potassium 705 mg

TIME

20 minutes preparation
30 minutes cooking

INGREDIENTS

1 ½ pounds veal cutlets, pounded thin
Salt and pepper to taste
½ cup all-purpose flour
5 tablespoons butter
¼ cup minced onion
1 tablespoon Hungarian paprika
¾ cup chicken broth, canned or fresh
½ teaspoon caraway seeds
¾ cup sour cream

Season cutlets with salt and pepper, then dredge lightly in flour. Shake off excess flour and reserve 2 tablespoons. In a skillet, heat butter and brown the cutlets quickly on both sides. Remove from skillet and keep warm.

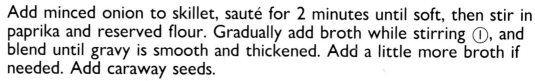

Add minced onion to skillet, sauté for 2 minutes until soft, then stir in paprika and reserved flour. Gradually add broth while stirring ①, and blend until gravy is smooth and thickened. Add a little more broth if needed. Add caraway seeds.

Return meat to skillet ②, cover, and simmer for 15 to 20 minutes until meat is tender. Blend in sour cream ③, and simmer mixture just until the sauce is heated through.

YIELD

4 servings

Per serving
calories 242, protein 6 g,
fat 11 g, sodium 257 mg,
carbohydrates 30 g,
potassium 720 mg

TIME

20 minutes preparation
2 hours chilling
30 minutes cooking

INGREDIENTS

1½ pounds white potatoes
2 tablespoons minced fresh parsley
1 clove garlic, crushed
Salt and pepper
2 tablespoons butter
1 tablespoon oil
⅓ cup grated Parmesan cheese

Scrub potatoes, place them in a saucepan, cover with cold water, bring to a boil, and simmer for 10 minutes. Drain and cool, then chill for 2 hours. Peel potatoes, then grate them coarsely into a bowl ①. Mix in parsley and garlic; season to taste with salt and pepper.

In a 7-inch nonstick skillet, heat butter and oil. Add potatoes, pack down ②, and smooth top and edges. Over medium heat, cook potatoes for about 7 minutes without stirring to brown the bottom. Shake the pan, and if you hear a rustling sound, the bottom is browned and crisp. Invert the cake onto a plate ③, then slide back into the skillet and brown the other side.

Slide the cake on a flameproof, flat serving dish. Sprinkle with grated cheese, then put under broiler to melt and lightly brown the cheese. Serve hot.

YIELD

6 servings

Per serving
calories 106, protein 9 g,
fat 6 g, sodium 1010 mg,
carbohydrates 5 g,
potassium 295 mg

TIME

20 minutes preparation
45 minutes cooking

INGREDIENTS

⅓ pound round or sirloin steak,
    thinly sliced
3 scallions
1 tablespoon oil
1 clove garlic, minced
3 tablespoons soy sauce
Pinch of red pepper flakes
Salt and pepper to taste
3 cups bean sprouts, washed and
    drained well
6 cups water
2 cups beef broth, canned or fresh

TOASTED SESAME SEEDS

¼ cup sesame seeds
Pinch of salt

First prepare the sesame seeds. Place seeds in a skillet and heat over medium heat until seeds are toast colored and puffed. Remove from the heat and sprinkle with salt. Place in a mortar or blender and pound or blend until seeds are pulverized ①. Reserve 1 teaspoon and place remainder in a glass jar for later use.

Cut the thinly sliced beef into 1-inch squares ②. Chop the white parts of the scallions; trim and reserve greens. In a saucepan, heat oil, add meat, white parts of scallions, garlic, 1 tablespoon soy sauce, red pepper flakes, and 1 teaspoon toasted sesame seeds; season with salt and pepper. Blend quickly and sauté over high heat for 1 minute, until meat is seared ③. Lower heat to medium and add the sprouts. Sauté, stirring a few times, for another 3 minutes.

Add the rest of the soy sauce and remaining ingredients except scallion tops, and blend well. Cook gently for about 30 minutes, until meat and sprouts are cooked. A few minutes before serving, shred the scallion tops and add to soup.

YIELD

4 servings

Per serving
calories 620, protein 63 g,
fat 27 g, sodium 532 mg,
carbohydrates 17 g,
potassium 1201 mg

TIME

30 minutes preparation
2 hours cooking

INGREDIENTS

3 tablespoons oil
2½ pounds sirloin tip or chuck roast,
    cut into ¾-inch slices
2 large onions, thinly sliced
2 cloves garlic, minced
Salt and pepper
4 sprigs fresh parsley
1 bay leaf
½ teaspoon dried leaf thyme
½ teaspoon dried marjoram

Pinch of grated nutmeg
1 cup beef broth, canned or fresh
1 tablespoon tomato paste
2 tablespoons red wine vinegar
3 cups beer or ale (approximately)
2 tablespoons cornstarch
3 tablespoons water

In a heavy skillet, heat oil over high heat. Sauté the beef slices quickly to brown on both sides ①. Remove from pan and reserve.

Reduce heat and sauté onions slowly until golden and soft. Add garlic and sauté 1 minute longer.

Cover the bottom of an ovenproof casserole with half the meat slices ②; season with a little salt and pepper, then cover with half the sautéed onions, the remaining beef, and then the rest of the onions.

Preheat oven to 325 degrees.

Tie parsley, bay leaf, thyme leaves, marjoram, and nutmeg in a piece of cheesecloth ③. Add to casserole, then add beef broth and tomato paste, vinegar, and enough beer or ale to just cover the meat and onions. Bring to a simmer on top of the stove, then place in hot oven and cook for about 1½ hours or until meat is tender. Remove meat from casserole to a serving dish and keep warm. Remove and discard cheesecloth bag with herbs.

Place casserole over moderately high heat. Let the sauce come to a simmer. Dissolve cornstarch in water, and add to the simmering sauce. Stir well and simmer until the sauce has thickened. Pour sauce over meat and serve.

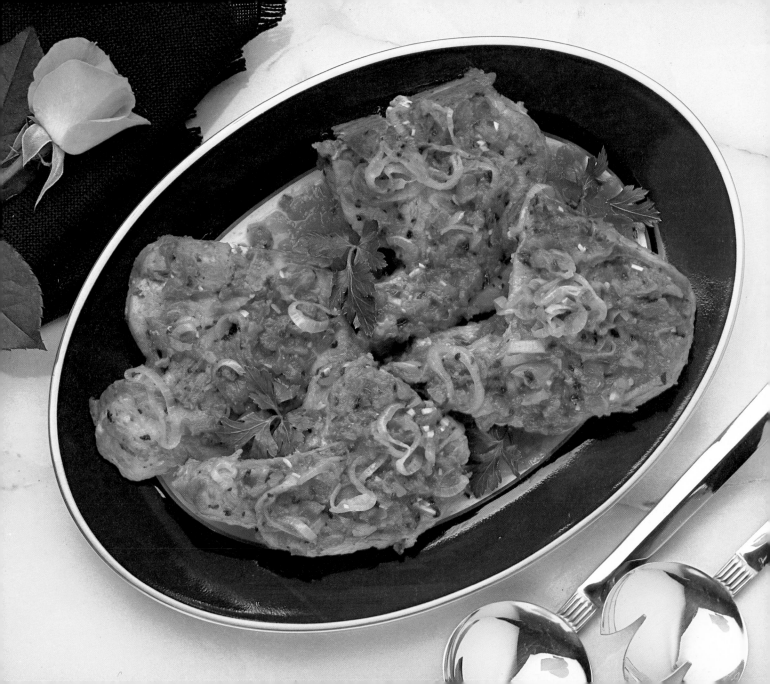

YIELD

4 servings

Per serving
calories 290, protein 25 g,
fat 18 g, sodium 382 mg,
carbohydrates 5 g,
potassium 587 mg

TIME

15 minutes preparation
1 hour cooking

INGREDIENTS

4 center-cut pork chops, about
    1¼ inches thick
Salt and pepper to taste
2 tablespoons olive oil
1 small onion, thinly sliced
1 large clove garlic, minced
1 cup canned tomatoes, drained and
    chopped

1 teaspoon chopped fresh basil leaves
    or ½ teaspoon dried
½ teaspoon dried oregano
¾ cup chicken broth, canned or fresh

Trim fat from the chops ①. Season chops with salt and pepper. In a heavy skillet, heat 1 tablespoon oil and brown chops on both sides ②. Remove chops and keep warm.

Discard fat and oil from skillet, add remaining tablespoon of oil, and sauté onion and garlic over moderate heat until limp and just starting to color. Add tomatoes, basil and oregano, and half the chicken broth. Stir well to deglaze the skillet ③.

Add pork chops to skillet, then cover skillet tightly. Cook slowly for about 45 minutes or until chops are tender. Turn chops once or twice during cooking and add more broth as needed.

YIELD

4 servings

Per serving
calories 514, protein 42 g,
fat 29 g, sodium 652 mg,
carbohydrates 13 g,
potassium 379 mg

TIME

10 minutes preparation
2 hours marinating
30 minutes cooking

INGREDIENTS

2 tablespoons lemon juice
¼ cup dark Jamaican rum
3 tablespoons soy sauce
1 tablespoon grated gingerroot
2 tablespoons grated onion
1 small clove garlic, crushed
½ teaspoon dried leaf thyme
Salt and pepper to taste
1 chicken, about 3 pounds, cut into
    serving pieces
½ cup all-purpose flour
½ cup oil

Combine and blend all ingredients except chicken, flour, and oil. Place chicken in a bowl, coat with marinating mixture ①, and let stand for 2 hours, turning the pieces a few times in the marinade.

Drain and dredge chicken in flour ②. Heat oil in a heavy skillet, then fry the chicken pieces over medium heat until well browned and tender ③, about 15 minutes. Turn once or twice during cooking.

YIELD

4 servings

Per serving
calories 273, protein 20 g,
fat 17 g, sodium 330 mg,
carbohydrates 9 g,
potassium 367 mg

TIME

15 minutes preparation
15 minutes cooking

INGREDIENTS

1 pound finely ground beef (top sirloin
   or sirloin tip)
1 cup finely diced peeled and boiled
   potatoes
2 egg yolks, lightly beaten
1/4 cup heavy cream
2 tablespoons minced onion
1/3 cup diced pickled beets
2 tablespoons capers, drained and
   chopped

1/2 teaspoon caraway seeds
Salt and pepper to taste
3 tablespoons butter

Combine ground meat, potatoes, eggs, and cream; blend well ①. Add remaining ingredients except butter. Mix and blend.

Shape mixture into 8 patties ②, each about 1/2 inch thick.

In a heavy skillet, melt butter and sauté patties quickly over high heat to brown on both sides ③.

YIELD

4 servings

Per serving
calories 308, protein 41 g, fat 11 g, sodium 354 mg, carbohydrates 9 g, potassium 1170 mg

TIME

15 minutes preparation
25 minutes cooking

INGREDIENTS

4 codfish or halibut steaks, about 2 pounds total
Salt and pepper to taste
3 tablespoons olive oil
1 medium onion, minced
1 large clove garlic, crushed
½ teaspoon dried leaf thyme
1 small bay leaf
1½ cups drained and chopped canned tomatoes

1 tablespoon minced fresh parsley
¼ teaspoon Tabasco
1 cup dry white wine

Wipe steaks with a damp cloth. Place in 1 layer in a buttered shallow baking dish ①. Set aside.

In a skillet, heat oil and sauté onion for 2 or 3 minutes until light golden ②. Add garlic and thyme, and sauté for another minute. Add tomatoes, stir well, and simmer for 2 minutes, then add the parsley, Tabasco, and wine. Mix, then simmer for 10 minutes until sauce has slightly thickened.

Preheat oven to 400 degrees.

Remove sauce from heat, and pour through a fine-meshed strainer ③. Spoon over fish in pan. Bake in hot oven for about 10 minutes, until fish is flaky and cooked.

YIELD

4 servings

Per serving
calories 529, protein 50 g,
fat 28 g, sodium 562 mg,
carbohydrates 19 g,
potassium 1357 mg

TIME

30 minutes preparation
1½ hours cooking

INGREDIENTS

4 tablespoons butter
2 pounds lean, boneless lamb, cut into
    1½-inch cubes
2 large carrots, pared and sliced ½
    inch thick
2 medium tomatoes, peeled, seeded,
    and chopped, or 2 canned
    tomatoes, drained
1 tablespoon tomato paste
12 very small white onions, peeled

1 cup green peas, fresh or frozen
1 teaspoon lemon juice
2 tablespoons chopped canned
    pimiento
¼ teaspoon hot red pepper flakes
Salt and pepper to taste
¾ cup chicken broth, canned or fresh
2 tablespoons chopped fresh dill, or 1
    tablespoon dillweed

In a saucepan, heat butter, and saute meat until lightly browned. Add carrot slices, and mix well ①. Reduce heat and cover tightly. Cook gently for about 1 hour, until all pan juices are absorbed; stir a few times to prevent scorching ②.

Add tomatoes, tomato paste, onions, peas (if frozen peas are used, instead add them 5 minutes before serving), lemon juice, pimiento, red pepper flakes, salt and pepper, and ⅓ cup chicken broth. Cover again and cook for another 30 minutes until meat is tender. Add more broth as needed ③. Add dill, stir, and simmer for another minute before serving.

YIELD

4 to 6 servings

Per serving (4)
calories 796, protein 43 g,
fat 61 g, sodium 1946 mg,
carbohydrates 14 g,
potassium 578 mg

TIME

25 minutes preparation
1 hour marinating
2½ hours cooking

INGREDIENTS

1 duckling, about 5 pounds
⅓ cup soy sauce
2 tablespoons dry sherry
2 tablespoons dark corn syrup
2 tablespoons grated onion
1 clove garlic, crushed
1 teaspoon grated gingerroot
½ teaspoon dry mustard
¼ teaspoon ground allspice
2 teaspoons cider vinegar

½ cup dry white wine
Salt and pepper to taste
2 teaspoons cornstarch mixed with 2
    tablespoons water

Remove any loose fat from duck cavity; rinse duck with cold water and dry with paper towel. Combine all other ingredients except cornstarch. Pour half the mixture into the duck cavity ①, coating the inner surface, then close the opening with skewers and string. Rub the remaining mixture into the duck skin ②, and let stand for 1 hour.

Preheat oven to 325 degrees.

Place duck on a rack in a roasting pan. Add 1 inch of water to the pan. Prick the duck skin in several places with a sharp fork. Roast in hot oven for 2 hours; add more water to pan if needed. Brush a few times with pan juices during roasting. After 2 hours, remove pan from oven, and remove trussing from duck. Let all juices from the cavity run into the pan. Pour pan juices into a bowl, remove rack, and place duck back into pan and roast for another 30 minutes.

Skim fat from the pan juices ③. A few minutes before the duck is done, place pan juices into a small saucepan, add the cornstarch mixture, and simmer while stirring until the sauce has thickened. Spoon sauce over the bird before serving.

YIELD

3 to 4 servings

Per serving (3)
calories 695, protein 37 g,
fat 55 g, sodium 1570 mg,
carbohydrates 11 g,
potassium 721 mg

TIME

15 minutes preparation
10 minutes cooking

INGREDIENTS

2 tablespoons butter
2 teaspoons olive oil
1 slice (about 1/4 pound)
  smoked ham, diced
2 Spanish sausages (chorizos) or 2
  Italian sausages, simmered 5
  minutes, then diced
1 medium potato, peeled and finely
  diced
6 eggs, lightly beaten

1 tablespoon minced fresh parsley
1 tablespoon minced scallions (white
  part only)
Salt and pepper to taste

In a skillet or omelette pan, heat 1 tablespoon butter and the olive oil; add diced ham and sausages, and sauté for about 2 minutes over medium heat until lightly browned ①. Remove ham and sausages and reserve. Add potato to pan; sauté while stirring until soft and golden brown. Combine eggs with parsley and scallions; season with salt and pepper. Stir in ham and sausages.

Pour egg mixture into the pan. Blend quickly with the potato and cook over moderate heat, shaking the pan a few times to prevent sticking. When the edge of the omelette starts to set, put the remaining butter on the edge of the omelette ② and tilt pan to let butter flow all around it ③. After about 2 minutes, put pan under a medium broiler to brown the top.

NOTE *This is an open-faced omelette and should not be folded.*

YIELD

4 servings

Per serving
calories 245, protein 17 g,
fat 17 g, sodium 260 mg,
carbohydrates 6 g,
potassium 308 mg

TIME

15 minutes preparation
10 minutes cooking

INGREDIENTS

¾ pound calves liver, or young steer
   liver, sliced very thin
2 tablespoons butter
2 tablespoons oil
1 large Spanish onion, sliced paper
   thin
Salt and pepper to taste
⅓ cup chicken broth, canned or fresh

Trim liver and remove all gristle or skin ①; cut into thin strips ②. In a skillet, heat butter and oil. Sauté onion slices over medium heat until soft and light golden—do not let brown. Remove onion to a plate and keep warm. Increase the heat under the skillet, and add liver slices. Sauté, shaking the pan a few times to prevent sticking, until liver is browned. This should take not longer than 2 minutes: the faster the liver is cooked, the tenderer it will be.

Return onion to skillet. Mix and heat through for half a minute, then season with salt and pepper. Remove liver and onions to a serving dish. Add broth to pan. Stir quickly to scrape up particles in pan and make a sauce. Spoon gravy over liver ③ and serve.

YIELD

4 servings

Per serving
calories 220, protein 44 g,
fat 2 g, sodium 1246 mg,
carbohydrates 4 g,
potassium 806 mg

TIME

5 minutes preparation
3 hours marinating
15 minutes cooking

INGREDIENTS

2 pounds haddock or cod fillets
3 tablespoons lemon juice
2 teaspoons salt
1 cup plain yogurt
1 teaspoon curry powder (or to taste)
1 large clove garlic, crushed
1 teaspoon grated gingerroot
$1/4$ teaspoon ground cardamom
$1/2$ teaspoon Tabasco (or to taste)

Pat fish fillets dry ①. Place fish in a flat glass or stainless dish, sprinkle on both sides with lemon juice and salt, and let stand for 10 minutes.

Blend remaining ingredients. Place fish in a shallow, oiled baking dish. Make 2 or 3 crosswise slashes in each fillet ②, then coat the entire surface with the yogurt mixture ③. Let stand for 3 hours.

Preheat oven to 375 degrees. Bake fish for about 15 minutes, or until flaky and done.

YIELD

6 servings

Per serving
calories 530, protein 46 g,
fat 28 g, sodium 964 mg,
carbohydrates 19 g,
potassium 861 mg

TIME

20 minutes preparation
1 hour, 45 minutes
   cooking

INGREDIENTS

4 pounds lean loin of pork
¼ cup all-purpose flour
1 tablespoon oil
1 large clove garlic, crushed
1 teaspoon salt
Black pepper to taste
2 tablespoons soy sauce
½ teaspoon powdered ginger
1½ tablespoons lime juice
3 pineapple rings, cut in half
3 tablespoons brown sugar

BASTING SAUCE

½ cup pineapple juice
3 tablespoons cider vinegar

Remove most fat from the meat; sprinkle lightly with flour ①. Heat oil in a large skillet or roasting pan, and brown pork quickly on all sides. Remove from pan and cool slightly.

Preheat the oven to 350 degrees.

Combine garlic, salt, pepper, soy sauce, ginger, and lime juice; rub mixture into the roast ②. Place meat in a roasting pan, rib side down, cook in hot oven for 25 minutes per pound, or about 1 hour, 45 minutes. About 30 minutes before roast is done, place pineapple rings on top ③, sprinkle with sugar, and finish cooking.

During cooking, baste roast a few times with the pineapple juice–vinegar mixture and the pan juices. Serve with pan gravy.

BEET BORSCHT (Russia)

YIELD

4 servings

Per serving
calories 288, protein 12 g,
fat 16 g, sodium 994 mg,
carbohydrates 23 g,
potassium 725 mg

TIME

20 minutes preparation
45 minutes cooking

INGREDIENTS

4 medium red beets
2 medium potatoes, peeled
1 medium onion
2 cups beef broth, canned or fresh
2 tablespoons lemon juice
1 teaspoon brown sugar
1 bay leaf
Salt and pepper to taste
½ pound smoked sausage (Kielbasa
    or other), cut into 1-inch slices

Wash and scrub beets; cut off tops ①. Place beets and potatoes in a saucepan, cover with water, and boil for about 15 minutes until beets are just soft enough to be pierced with a toothpick. Remove beets and potatoes from water; slip skins off beets ②. Strain the cooking water and reserve 3 cups.

Coarsely grate beets, potatoes and onion into a saucepan ③. Add reserved cooking liquid, beef broth, lemon juice, sugar, and bay leaf; season with salt and pepper. Bring to a boil, add the sliced sausage, cover, and simmer for about 30 minutes until vegetables are very soft.

YIELD

4 servings

Per serving

calories 519, protein 35 g,
fat 33 g, sodium 615 mg,
carbohydrates 19 g,
potassium 1029 mg

TIME

20 minutes preparation
45 minutes cooking

INGREDIENTS

1 tablespoon olive oil
¾ pound lean ground pork
¾ pound ground beef
½ cup chopped onion
1 large clove garlic, minced
1 cup tomato purée
¼ cup beef broth, canned or fresh
¼ cup raisins, soaked in water
   and drained
¼ cup coarsely chopped
   blanched almonds

1 tablespoon chili powder (or to taste)
½ teaspoon Tabasco (or to taste)
2 tablespoons sliced pimiento-stuffed
   olives
1 tablespoon chopped fresh parsley
Pinch of ground cinnamon
2 whole cloves
2 teaspoons sugar
2 teaspoons lemon juice
Salt and pepper to taste

Heat oil in a skillet or heavy saucepan; add the chopped meats, blend well, and break up clumps with a fork ①. Brown the meat lightly, then add onion and garlic ②. Sauté for another minute. Add tomato purée and broth ③, bring to a simmer, blend in all other ingredients, cover, and simmer for 30 minutes. Stir a few times, and add more broth if mixture is too dry. Serve with rice or as a filling for tacos.

FISH TERIYAKI (Japan)

YIELD

4 servings

Per serving
calories 487, protein 44 g,
fat 28 g, sodium 1498 mg,
carbohydrates 4 g,
potassium 1046 mg

TIME

5 minutes preparation
20 minutes marinating
20 minutes cooking

INGREDIENTS

4 tablespoons Japanese soy sauce
4 tablespoons mirin (see note)
4 tablespoons sake or dry sherry
1 clove garlic, crushed
1 teaspoon grated gingerroot
4 pieces mackerel fillet, or tuna or
    bluefish (about 2 pounds total)

Place all ingredients except fish in a saucepan. Bring to a boil and simmer for 1 minute. Remove from heat and allow to cool.

Place mixture in a bowl, add fish, stir to coat well ①, and marinate for 20 minutes. Drain fish and reserve marinade.

Preheat the broiler. Place fish in the broiler pan ②, and grill for about 5 minutes per side, depending on the thickness of the pieces. Brush 4 or 5 times during broiling with reserved marinade ③. When cooked, the fish should have a deep brown, shiny glaze.

NOTE Mirin is a sweet cooking rice wine, available in many supermarkets on their oriental food shelves and in all oriental food stores. If mirin is not available, add more dry sherry to the marinade and also add 1 tablespoon sugar.

YIELD

4 servings

Per serving
calories 354, protein 27 g,
fat 15 g, sodium 698 mg,
carbohydrates 27 g,
potassium 793 mg

TIME

20 minutes preparation
1 hour standing
30 minutes cooking

INGREDIENTS

1 pound lean ground lamb
3/4 cup minced onion
1 clove garlic, minced
3/4 cup soft white bread crumbs
1 large egg, lightly beaten
1 tablespoon lemon juice
1/4 teaspoon ground cinnamon
1/3 cup chopped fresh parsley
Salt and pepper to taste
1/2 cup all-purpose flour

3 tablespoons butter
1 1/2 cups tomato sauce mixed
  with about 1/4 cup water

In a bowl, combine meat, onion, garlic, and bread crumbs. Mix with a fork, then work in egg, lemon juice, cinnamon, and parsley; season with salt and pepper. Shape the mixture into small balls ①, then flatten them slightly ② and sprinkle very lightly with flour ③.

Preheat oven to 350 degrees.

In a skillet, heat butter, and brown the meat quickly—for about 1 to 2 minutes. Place the patties in a shallow baking dish, cover with tomato sauce mixture. Place in hot oven for 30 minutes to finish cooking.

BRAISED CHICKEN WINGS (China)

YIELD

4 servings

Per serving
calories 367, protein 25 g,
fat 24 g, sodium 2065 mg,
carbohydrates 11 g,
potassium 291 mg

TIME

15 minutes preparation
30 minutes cooking

INGREDIENTS

2 pounds chicken wings
3 tablespoons cooking oil
6 tablespoons soy sauce
2 tablespoons dry sherry
1½ tablespoons honey
2 scallions (green and white parts),
    sliced
1 clove garlic, minced
¼ teaspoon freshly ground pepper

Cut wings through joints ①. Discard the wing tips or use for making chicken broth. In a skillet or wok, heat oil, and fry the chicken over high heat until nicely browned on both sides, about 3 or 4 minutes ②.

Combine all other ingredients. Pour off all but about 1 tablespoon fat from skillet, then add the mixture of ingredients, and coat the wing pieces with the mixture. Cover the skillet, reduce heat, and cook for about 25 minutes, or until the chicken is tender. Turn the pieces once during cooking and stir a few times to prevent the sauce from burning ③. When done, the chicken should be nicely glazed and practically no liquid left in the skillet.

YIELD

4 servings

Per serving
calories 582, protein 52 g,
fat 22 g, sodium 846 mg,
carbohydrates 42 g,
potassium 1998 mg

TIME

30 minutes preparation
1 hour, 15 minutes
   cooking

INGREDIENTS

2 pounds lean pork (shoulder or butt)
2 tablespoons butter
2 medium onions, sliced thin
1 white turnip, pared and diced
2 large carrots, pared and diced
2 stalks celery (white part only), sliced
1 bay leaf
1 teaspoon dried marjoram

Pinch of dried thyme
1 teaspoon lemon juice
Salt and pepper to taste
2½ cups chicken broth
   (approximately), canned or fresh
4 large potatoes, peeled and diced

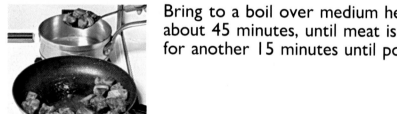

Trim most fat and any skin off the meat. Cut into 1½-inch cubes ①. In a heavy skillet, heat butter, and brown the pork. Remove from skillet and place in a saucepan ②.

Add onions, turnip, carrots, and celery to saucepan. Mix well, then add bay leaf, marjoram, thyme, and lemon juice; season with salt and pepper. Add enough chicken broth to barely cover the ingredients ③.

Bring to a boil over medium heat, cover, reduce heat, and simmer for about 45 minutes, until meat is nearly cooked. Add potatoes, and cook for another 15 minutes until potatoes are cooked.

INDEX